Racism

Lord Loveday Ememe

By Lord Loveday Ememe and available from Lulu and Amazon

The Constitution and policing

Heresy

Starfleet

The Supernatural

Creation

Deterrence

Stalking

The Media

Adam

Criminal Responsibility

The Wicked

Common Law

www.lulu.com

Copyright© Lord Loveday Ememe 2015

The author asserts the moral right to be recognized as the author of this work.
ISBN: 978-1-326-38053-3

Table of Contents

1. The persecution of the law

2. The Creation of the United Nations and its purpose

3. What is policing

4. Author's notes

5. Author's biography

6. Bibliography

1. The persecution of the law

What is racism? Racism is the persecution of the law, the civil noble constitution, by supernatural beings. It is the misuse of supernatural powers and senses to harm the civil noble constitution mentally or physically or to breach the peace in a civilized society. Real racism is what real crime is, real racism is real lawlessness, and real lawlessness is real madness. Real racism is beyond the capabilities of the civil noble constitution; only supernatural beings are capable of real racism because of their supernatural powers and senses.

Racism is the conspiracy of supernatural beings to directly or indirectly undermine the regulatory authority of the civil noble constitution. This is best achieved by the criminalization of the civil noble constitution by the misuse of supernatural powers and senses with spells etcetera.

Racism is the deliberate misuse of supernatural powers and senses to create conditions on this planet that do not support life, conditions that cater to the wicked hostile nature of the supernatural constitution that do not have universal application. The standard that is used to determine if the conditions on a planet support life is if the conditions meet all the needs of the civil noble constitution, all the real civil rights of the civil noble constitution are satisfied. This has universal application.

Racism is when supernatural beings go on strike from fulfilling their sacred obligations to the state, the civil noble constitution, because of their obsession to be worshiped by the civil noble constitution, by building mosques, synagogues, churches etcetera.

Racism is when supernatural beings undermine the common law rights and privileges of the civil noble lord and the protocols established because of their uncivilized constitutions when having contact or communicating with the civil noble lord. This also includes making the price too high, at a cost, for the civil noble lord, with regard to not having suitable female companions because of their uncivilized constitutions, taking for granted the necessary training or education to be ladies to become suitable companions for the civil noble lord.

It is an additional persecution of the law, the civil noble constitution, a racist attack, when supernatural beings try to include the civil noble constitution in punishments meant for supernatural beings for not fulfilling their sacred obligations to the state, the civil noble constitution.

Supernatural beings are uncivilized naturally and as a consequence are required to behave appropriately to be law abiding or civilized, this includes fulfilments of their obligations to the state which requires different types of routines. This is different for the civil noble constitution who is civilized naturally whose natural behaviour cannot be unlawful whose official role as law lord or ruler does not require routine. This does not mean that being a law lord is not demanding, on the contrary, it is very demanding in ways that are beyond the comprehension of supernatural beings. It is a serious crime, a racist attack, for supernatural beings to include unlawfully compulsory routine in the official role of a real ruler.

It is generally believed especially in Greek mythology that gods do what they like including the misuse of supernatural powers and senses and still expect to be revered or venerated. There is some truth in this but it is not supernatural gods but civil gods. My experience confirms that supernatural beings believe wrongly that this applies to them. It does not; supernatural beings are criminally responsible because of their supernatural powers and senses and are expected to behave responsibly because of the potentially destructive nature of their supernatural powers and senses when misused.

It is a racist attack when supernatural beings try to force the civil noble constitution to have conversations with them that are based on a false reality, a reality that unlawfully promotes or advocates lawlessness, the unlawful supremacy of the supernatural constitution. Supernatural beings while pretending to be of a constitution they are not, the civil noble constitution, portray the civil constitution as wicked, incompetent, illiterate etcetera and the civil system as flawed or inadequate, a racist sabotage of the sacred determination made that the civil constitution is the rule, ruler. This is the dumb criminal syndrome unique to the supernatural constitution; they do not know what a real ruler is or its real purpose and are constantly making themselves appear ridiculous, demonic. This is the same way they undermined the Christian teachings which identify the civil noble constitution as the rule, ruler; a sacred determination that has never been put into practice. They misapplied the Christian teachings which led to the abomination of the creation of churches and the unlawful supremacy of the supernatural constitution, the creation of hell on earth.

If you compare the civil and supernatural constitutions it will become immediately apparent that the civil constitution has been naturally regulated or restricted or taxed for sacred regulatory purposes as ruler, no further direct or indirect regulation, restriction or taxation of the civil constitution is permitted, this serves a regulatory purpose. Supernatural beings that undermine this sacred determination are racist that are trying to undermine the regulatory authority of the civil noble constitution.

The protocols, procedures or processes developed for the security of the civil constitution as protection from the uncivilized wicked nature of the supernatural constitution, are now being used as weapons by supernatural beings to harm the civil constitution mentally and physically which is referred to as bureaucratic red tape.

Companionship, sexual intercourse is traditionally a civil right for the righteous. The civil constitution has naturally fulfilled all the necessary traditional rites to have any supernatural female or to have supernatural females as companions. This does not apply to supernatural males; they are required to behave appropriately to be law abiding in order to fulfil the traditional rites to have female companions. To undermine this sacred determination made regarding companionship is a racist attack on the civil noble constitution.

Racist supernatural beings prefer the current practice of the demonic supernatural demonstration of the law, supernatural methods, rather than the sacred requirement or determination, the immediate application of the law through the civil noble constitution as ruler, the rule.

Supernatural beings have associated their supernatural powers and senses with being blessings from God, gifts, at the expense of the civil noble constitution, who is not blessed or gifted. These blessings they claim extend to good looks, the physical appearance, including the size of the penis at the expense of the civil noble constitution to the extent of having the audacity to interfere with the civil noble constitution's physical appearance etcetera. These misconceptions are linked to their unlawful misapplication of the Christian teachings facilitating the unlawful supremacy of the supernatural constitution resulting in lawlessness.

The god complex, superiority complex attitude of the supernatural constitution towards the civil noble constitution that has been the case for centuries or for millennia, the result of the misapplication of the Christian teachings and the taking for granted of the common law protocols, the common law rights and privileges of the civil noble constitution, has made it almost impossible for the supernatural constitution to be law abiding or understand what it means to be law abiding. An amusing interpretation of being law abiding is to pretend to be a constitution they are not, the civil constitution, and neglecting their sacred obligations to the state, the civil noble constitution, as the working class. Another amusing interpretation is to invade the privacy of the noble lord, a supernatural method, under the guise of concern or help or assistance. These different unlawful contradictory attempts at submission to the law are because of the damage they did to themselves by requiring the law, the civil noble constitution, to worship them. It is a desperate attempt to avoid the inevitable by exploring every option but the right one. Even to the extent of ending the life of the civil noble lord by treating the noble lord as having a medical disability or an inanimate object rather than a ruler.

This racist god complex attitude affects the official recognition of the civil noble lord as commissioner of the metropolitan police force with the allowance or salary. The livery of the law lord is dominated by the blue colour, the blue colour is associated with law and order, the purpose of the uniform is to be identified with the law lord, the civil noble constitution that despite the differences there is a uniformity of purpose under the leadership of the civil noble lord.

The implications of any country on this planet referring to the supernatural constitution as its rule or ruler, whether or not the supernatural being pretends to be of a civil constitution, is to admit that the country advocates lawlessness, hell on earth and the unlawful persecution of the law the civil noble constitution.

The revelation of racism in the Garden of Eden after the identification of the civil noble constitution as the law, paradise or heaven and the failure of the supernatural constitution because of the harsh hostile living conditions in the Garden of Eden, confirm that the role of the civil noble lord as ruler is very important and must be taken seriously by supernatural beings. The consequences of undermining the regulatory authority of the civil noble constitution or treating the kingship of the civil noble constitution as tokenism are extremely severe, hell on earth. A real ruler has very serious applications although not tokenism it is ceremonial in its application because of the nature of the civil noble constitution. Its application has the semblance of symbolism, I use the word symbolism because of the standard employed today by supernatural beings that are not real rulers. The civil constitution represents no work, peace and security. The civil noble constitution represents the standard supernatural beings should aspire to in order to ensure peace and security. The civil noble constitution works in a different unconventional sacrificial way, which are undermined or taken for granted by supernatural beings. The role of a real ruler compared to the standard employed today by supernatural beings unlawfully pretending to be rulers will appear to be stationary or statue-like.

The civil noble constitution is or was not meant to know what death, old age (ageing), diseases, poverty are, these are punishments for the criminally responsible, the civil noble constitution is not criminally responsible. It is racism to make the civil noble constitution experience these punishments meant only for the criminally responsible.

When supernatural beings unlawfully pretend to be of civil noble constitutions and advocate lifestyles that are beyond the capabilities of the civil noble constitution, for example, education and training, healthcare provisions, lifespan, wealth acquisition, poverty, languages etcetera it is racism, racist attacks on the civil noble constitution.

The more advanced a civilization the less significant the supernatural constitution becomes, given the natural domineering nature of the supernatural constitution, an advanced civilization will not be readily acceptable.

The law protects the supernatural constitution from the wicked actions of other supernatural beings because the law, the civil noble constitution, has dominion over this planet. The supernatural constitution cannot disassociate its supernatural powers and senses from its constitution, and will be in breach of the peace when offensive towards another supernatural being even when supernatural powers and senses have not been directly used. Breach of the peace involves the misuse of supernatural powers and senses and it is racism in the dominion of the civil noble constitution. Supernatural beings have collectively decided that relationships with them, contrary to the provisions made by common law, are dependent on which political party is in government. Whether they are family, girl friends etcetera, their relationships with the civil noble constitution are dependent on which supernatural political party is in government. They behave like robots with no soul. Their attitudes toward the civil noble constitution are dependent on which supernatural political party is in government. This vindicates the determination made by international and domestic legislations that refuse to acknowledge or accept or recognize the supernatural constitution in any relationship with the civil noble constitution. Supernatural beings are not recognized or accepted as legal persons. The supernatural political lifespan linked to lawlessness including supernatural political experiences linked to lawlessness like illnesses, ageing etcetera do not apply to the civil noble constitution whose lifespan and experiences have been clearly defined and legalized linked to natural righteousness. When supernatural beings try to directly or indirect compromise these sacred civil rights of the civil noble constitution it is racism.

Given the sacred description or definition of a ruler, which is the civil noble constitution, when supernatural beings refer to a supernatural being as a ruler in the dominion of the civil noble constitution in the media it is deception or an attempt at deceiving the legal viewer or viewers or the legal listener or listeners, casting spells on the vulnerable.

There is a difference between not wanting to violate the right to privacy of the civil noble constitution, the law lord, and lying to or deceiving the civil noble constitution. To lie to a law lord by a supernatural being is interpreted as casting a spell on the noble lord by common law which is a criminal offence. A court of law is the dominion of the law lord and to lie to the court the noble lord given the sacred sacrificial nature of a real law lord for regulatory purposes is a serious crime which will be interpreted as casting a spell on the civil noble constitution.

The civil noble constitution is not naturally political, it is a legal constitution, but remains a political prisoner in a lawless political world. The civil noble constitution in a political lawless system or systems of government is a political prisoner which is interpreted by common law as being under one type of spell or another, directly or indirectly, from supernatural beings during the duration of these lawless political governments that undermine the existence or continued existence of the civil noble constitution, the law.

2. The creation of the United Nations and its purpose

The United Nations is a police force; its development has been very slow because it is a process that encompasses the education of what a real police force is and the definition of crime. The creation of the United Nations is linked to the most notorious racist in history Hitler and his Nazis regime, a regime that advocated the supremacy of the Aryan race, the persecution of others of the same race because they were Jewish or disabled.

Whether the Second World War was role play by supernatural beings or not, it does not change the fact that the United Nations was established as a consequence, a police force with a clear mandate, the total elimination of real racism. The elimination of real racism is the sacred objective of the United Nations; real racism is the unlawful persecution of the law, the civil noble constitution. The Jews during the Second World War represented the righteous children of God a fictional representation of the civil noble constitution, the Nazi regime a fictional representation of supernatural beings.

The police service and the civil service in the United Kingdom are meant to operate without any political affiliations in the delivery of services; their workers are not allowed to be influenced by their political afflictions. The supernatural constitution is political by nature and does not fit into the legal description of a person for the purposes of working for or the facilitation of these services. Yet the obstruction of the United Nations operating as a police service is the contradictory criterion that countries have to have a democratic political government, to be political to be part of the police service, the United Nations.

The United Nations in its undeveloped incomplete stage is operating politically illegally facilitating the activities as a police service it is meant stop.

Politics or democracy is discriminatory, a group or groups of people are always discriminated against. An African musician Fela Kuti referred to democracy as the demonstration of craziness. It is insanity to advocate or campaign with lawlessness or discrimination as the objective of a political party when elected to govern.

The supernatural constitution is naturally political and does not fit the non-discriminatory objective or mandate of a police force, as a consequence can only join a police force or service under the commission and guidance of the civil noble constitution.

The Security Council is the United Nations' most powerful body; its primary responsibility is the maintenance of international peace and security. Five powerful countries sit as permanent members with ten elected members with two-year terms. The composition and operation are racist, discriminatory, a contradiction to the purpose of a real police service. The Security Council is dominated by the white race, which will suggest that Hitler succeeded indirectly what he could not directly. This advocates the supremacy of the supernatural constitution with the necessary imbalance to maintain demonism under the guise of policing. The claim to have earned the right to be permanent members of the Security Council is because of the deception of advanced civilizations, which in fact are organized barbarisms. There are no civilized countries on this planet.

A police service must have a clearly defined mandate which is not vulnerable to change or political manipulations or public opinion. Politics or democracy is revolutionary, revolution against an established order.

The civil noble constitution as law lord has been sacredly constituted to be a sacred database for the defined mandate of the police service. The police service cannot be commissioned by a political process even more so by a political process based on a lie a false reality.

The political democratic system of government as a method or process of establishing a police service, the United Nations, is similar in principle but worse than requiring prisoners to vote on who will be the prison warden or administrator and prison officers, they will prefer outlaws to fill these positions, so that the real criminal traits of prisoners will be overlooked at the expense of rehabilitation which undermines real law and order.

The wrong interpretation of the Christian teachings refers to an Angel as a supernatural being with supernatural behaviour and manifestations commissioned by a supernatural being. The correct interpretation of the Christian teachings refers to an Angel as a supernatural being with civil behaviour and manifestations, uniform, commissioned by a civil noble lord.

It is amusing when supernatural beings try to give a racist explanation or justification for supernatural racist attacks on the vulnerable. The use of the words amusing or comedy to describe the wicked actions of supernatural beings is not to trivialize the wicked acts but to confirm the determination made that demons suffer from dumb criminal syndrome.

As a consequence of the wicked hostile nature of the supernatural constitution, supernatural beings treat very serious life issues like death, illness, poverty, wealth, the role of the civil noble lord, crime, as jokes and games to play. The incomplete constitution of the United Nations, the police service, has made it political an institution of ridicule used to undermine these serious life issues, unlawfully by supernatural beings.

Although the church represents the wrong interpretation and application of the Christian teachings it does provide some insight into how to deal with supernatural beings behaving unlawfully, the situation should be dealt with by other supernatural beings in the same way an armed response unit in the United Kingdom, the metropolitan force, responds to the commission of a crime with firearms that unarmed police officers do not deal with.

Privatization and nationalization have been the main distinction of political parties unlawfully endorsed by the United Nations, the police service; nationalization has been deceptively referred to as the socialist red ideology by supernatural beings unlawfully masquerading as civilized, of civil constitutions, and privatization theft as blue capitalist ideology. The revelation of the differences between the civil and supernatural constitutions makes nationalization blue the representation of the civil noble constitution and privatization theft a representation of the supernatural constitution.

Privatization generates problems with the environment like transportation, owning cars; public transport in the United Kingdom is up to the necessary standard to make car ownership unnecessary. Only state officials can have official cars for security purposes and it protects the civil noble constitution from the strange unique interest from supernatural beings. Unfortunately privatization is political, it encourages fighting the domination of the vulnerable, it encourages unfairness with the distribution of natural resources. It is an ingenious representation of some of the regulatory compensatory legal needs of the civil noble constitution as political, hostile, to undermine the law. It is not right, that because the state is meant to provide services, food, healthcare, housing, transportation etcetera that the quality or the quality of life should not be better than that currently enjoyed by billionaires today.

The problem with state services has been that the products and services are substandard compared to the private sector. Why is this the case? It is simply sabotage, to undermine the state, the law, by the conspiracy of supernatural beings.

The real problem with access or delivery of services is the wicked nature of the supernatural constitution. This is why the rule is the civil constitution for purposes of professionalism, which is enforced through science and technology. Supernatural beings try to sabotage technological advancements in order to give themselves something to do with horrific consequences because of their wicked constitutions. The lawless cultures all around the world today that had been the case for millennia are characterizations of the supernatural constitution. Supernatural beings can never be commissioners of a legitimate police service which accounts for the incomplete political nature of the United Nations.

A police service established for any purpose other than for the protection of the civil noble constitution, as commissioner, to uphold the law, has a political discriminatory agenda and will meet resistance. The civil noble constitution is not criminally responsible and as a consequence accountable to nobody, to treat the civil noble constitution as if a criminal whether as a joke or a game or not as a joke or a game by supernatural beings is political and a racist attack. It will undermine the sacred objectives of the police service and will undermine law and order. This is the real reason a police force will be referred to as institutionally racist a contradiction to its sacred objectives.

If the police service is operating legally for legal purposes it does not need consensus, a political process for support, if the police service is operating illegally for illegal purposes it needs consensus a political process for support, which is the current way the United Nations in its current undeveloped state operates.

In the bible john 8:7 it was written that Jesus Christ said to a group of people that were trying to punish a prostitute, he that is without sin among you, let him first cast a stone at her. This suggests that it is only the righteous, the civil noble constitution, that can commission a police service for lawful purposes.

The police service while providing goods and services must be guided by the lesson in the Garden of Eden, technological advancements for the provision of goods and services must not be supernatural but civilized to avoid the apple tree incident with Lord Adam.

There is a very strange deception by supernatural beings regarding knowledge and its link to the supernatural with regard to the apple tree in the Garden of Eden; some refer to the tree as the knowledge of good and evil. Some interpret this incident as justification to obstruct the education or the development of the civil noble constitution for political lawless purposes. Lord Adam was initially educated about good and evil by unlawfully being told not to eat from a tree in his dominion. The real lesson I believe is how the civil noble constitution as king obtains knowledge. Do you compromise the civil noble constitution by altering or converting the civil noble constitution from civil noble constitution to supernatural constitution to obtain knowledge supernaturally? Or do you educate or train the civil noble constitution in a civilized legal manner without altering the civil noble constitution? You educate the civil noble constitution in a civilized legal manner without altering the civil noble constitution, respectfully because the civil constitution is king and a sacredly delicate constitution.

A real police service is sacred with a sacred objective, the total elimination of real racism, and real racism is the persecution of the law, the civil noble constitution, directly or indirectly; this is emphasized by the sacred requirement that the essential component of the construction of a real police service is the civil noble constitution, the law, as commissioner of police.

The civil noble constitution as commissioner of police is permanent and cannot be undermined by supernatural beings, even though Lord Adam's civil noble constitution was unlawfully compromised by the conspiracy of supernatural beings, he remains a law lord a commissioner of police although incapacitated and cannot function as a law lord. He was created civilized originally of a civil noble constitution and continues to remain entitled to have his original constitution restored, the unlawful conversion corrected. This does not apply to supernatural beings that were born or created supernatural because of the existence of the supernatural creator when Lord Adam was created.

Unfortunately because of the circumstances that led to the unlawful overthrow of the civil noble constitution in the Garden of Eden, the civil noble constitution never emerged as the sacred ruler that the civil noble constitution is, as a consequence remains a childlike being, and is always referred to as the son of God rather than God. The unfortunate compromise of the dignity of the noble lord by the conspiracy of supernatural beings remains the way the noble lord is perceived and remains a political victory for the supernatural constitution which has no legal significance. The police service must correct this anomaly in the interest of law and order, international peace and security.

Supernatural beings try to hide behind concern regarding accountability to justify undermining the civil noble constitution's rightful position as ruler. They first need to understand the real duties of a ruler and the extent of the differences between the civil and supernatural constitutions. The civil noble constitution is not criminally responsible. Common law also provides the answer, the United Kingdom parliament, the House of Commons and the House of Lords, the monarch although commissioner of the government is not held accountable for their actions. This is based on the true nature of a real monarch and the true nature of the real working class. The true nature of the real working class the supernatural constitution, they got what they voted for or they got what they allowed to happen. Unfortunately the United Nations is currently operating as a discriminatory racist political service rather than a police service or law enforcement agency.

3. What is policing

Policing is the upholding or protection of the law, the law in living form, the civil noble constitution. This involves the protection of all the fundamental human rights of the civil noble constitution. These rights are really the king's rights, keeping the king's peace. Unfortunately reverence for the civil noble constitution by supernatural beings is essential to policing; it is an important component for the regulation of supernatural beings. The civil noble constitution is the law in living form.

If the United Nations, the police service, is not aware of these fundamentals of policing, that the civil noble constitution, the law, is the police service then it is institutionally racist, a racist organization and a contradiction to the sacred objective of the police service which is the immediate effective total elimination of racism.

The institution of the law, the civil noble constitution, provides the immediate protection of everyone creating international peace and security.

Policing starts within the police service itself, to be precise, the chain of command, supernatural police officers submitting to the law, the civil noble constitution as commissioner of police. Supernatural beings that want to use the law the civil noble constitution as an inanimate object or a ghost or as a being with a medical condition rather than the law, commissioner of police, are racists, saboteurs of the sacred objective of the police service.

The failsafe sacred protection of the civil noble constitution from the hostile nature of the uncivilized supernatural constitution preventing deviation from the sacred common law protocols, submission to the law, the undermining of these sacred protocols constitutes making the life of the civil noble constitution hell unlawfully, which will then trigger the civil noble lord's sacred legal right of vengeance, the condemnation to hell of the wicked the retaliatory effects of the wicked given the differences between the civil and supernatural constitutions.

Effective policing requires clarity starting with the civil noble constitution; racists expect the civil noble constitution to assimilate information supernaturally, to solve a puzzle, rather than things being explained properly. Information should be given as if being given to the civil noble constitution. This means that the standard is clarity and not confusion which is a racist attack.
Policing is undermined when supernatural beings dismiss or disregard the law, the civil noble constitution, as a medical disability for political lawless purposes.
For security and policing purposes the civil noble constitution must be identified officially as commissioner of police, it cannot be a secret, to prevent supernatural political manipulations of the law. This is separate from the protected right to privacy of the civil noble constitution.
Uncivilized practices by supernatural beings even when done out of sight of real nobles are unlawful because uncivilized behaviour by a supernatural being is similar to a recovering alcoholic and alcohol in most cases it will get out of control and represent an unacceptable threat to real nobles and in a civilized society.
Germany was suspended from full participation in United Nations international peace keeping operations because of the determination made that their past behaviour the instigation of two world wars undermined international peace and security. This is correct in principle with regard to the destabilization of the world with the exportation of democracy the political discriminatory persecutory culture racism that persecutes the law, the civil noble constitution, by the white race. I am of a civil noble constitution and always racially abused by Caucasians. When I try to access services, I discover that they have been unlawfully supernaturally rigged by Caucasians to be the ones to provide the services and I am constantly racially attacked by them in the process of the provision of these services. Democracy the participation of supernatural beings in the political process is

poisonous to the supernatural constitution similar to a recovering alcoholic and alcohol. I believe that Caucasians should be excluded from leading roles in a properly constituted police service.

Politics or the political discriminatory process, democracy, is the revolution of the uncivilized against an established order, the law. It obviously compromises policing and has the latent subtle effect of triggering the forbidden god complex superiority complex self-destructive trait of the supernatural constitution. It is a poison that is meant to destroy supernatural beings, although it is not the initial impression it gives. It is the real forbidden fruit. The destruction of the supernatural constitution is gradual, it first attacks the self-control of the supernatural constitution by creating the addiction to interfere with other people and how they live their lives. The supernatural constitution constantly wants to have a say in how others live their lives, they will initially try to justify this nosey interest morally until that ceases to be relevant. They then try to create problems in the lives of their victims to justify the nosey interest until that ceases to be valid, then, the open madness of interference or nosey interest, to cater to the nosey nature of the supernatural constitution, all these problems because of revolting against their medication, the law and proper policing.

For purposes of security and policing the uncivilized or supernatural beings are not allowed to socialize with the civil noble constitution, informality is a political sabotage of the regulatory authority of the civil noble constitution. Every situation involving supernatural beings having contact or communicating with the civil noble lord must be formal in the civil noble lord's capacity as ruler with the necessary protocols because of the uncivilized wicked nature of the supernatural constitution. This is further emphasized by the sacred determination, common law, that the companions of the civil noble lord must be ladies with extensive training in etiquette. Ladies are really strictly companions of the civil noble lord. The training of a lady is tailored to meet the needs of a real lord, the civil noble constitution.

A mad person is not aware of a dangerous situation; the supernatural constitution is wicked partly because of the lack of awareness of hostile situations and the creation of hostile situations.

Supernatural beings of all skin colours have conspired to mortgage the lives of the vulnerable including the lives of nobles to play gods at certain periods under lawless discriminatory political systems of government.

What are the fundamental human rights essential to policing? The most important of these rights is the right to life. This right includes quality of life, life span. Healthcare is an integral component of this sacred right to life. The life span of the civil noble constitution is immortality, this extends to supernatural beings and for supernatural beings this right is dependent on good behaviour contrary to the misinterpretation of the Christian teachings that it is the other way round.

The right to privacy is an important civil right of the civil noble constitution given the intrusive nature of the supernatural constitution. This right protects the civil noble constitution from the wicked nature of the supernatural constitution, the supernatural senses of sight and hearing. This right is reinforced by other civil rights, the right to freedom of expression and the right to freedom of speech, supernatural beings are natural bullies that try to force themselves on the vulnerable through intimidation or oppression as the charm associated with good behaviour is beyond their capabilities. They like to unlawfully control what you do or say when you are in the privacy of your home when they unlawfully try to force relationships with you supernaturally unlawfully similar to rape or paedophilia given the differences between the civil and supernatural constitutions. This is evident with the unlawful alterations to films and music, supernatural beings through this think they can get around the protected civil rights of the civil noble constitution. The voices in music and the images in films have been altered to be live and supernatural contrary to the trade description legislations.

There is the stalking use of their supernatural powers and senses, they initially try to create the impression of concern or help which contradicts their past and present atrocities, which gradually develops into attempts at humiliation or embarrassment to control future forced unlawful contacts or communications while at the same time make it appear voluntary, the sadism of suffering in silence without making any complaints. This stalking racist interest is also evident anytime I try to paint my home, they simulate problems that occur in a desert in extreme conditions when the wind blows sand into a room or as if the room caught fire, they supernaturally turn the walls brown minutes after painting. The simulation of an event without the actual event occurring but with the permanent result of the event as if it actually occurred. Things people buy that do not develop problems, they change or throw away in their own time, it is different in my case, these things are damaged supernaturally as is of wear and tear without the event but a simulation of it with the permanent result of the event as if it occurred. Stalking is an unwanted interest from racist supernatural beings because of its tortuous effects on their victims. The civil right to privacy is constant for the civil noble constitution because the noble lord is not criminally responsible, for supernatural beings this right is dependent on good behaviour which can be suspended for purposes of national security or policing because supernatural beings are criminally responsible.

On the fourth of July 2015, I was subjected to sustained supernatural attacks in the form of thunder and lightening in front of my house, this has been my experience for over twelve years at this property. These are attacks by supernatural beings or being with a god complex. I am a very private person of a civil noble constitution and I do not socialize with supernatural beings because they are too uncivilized for my taste. This means that the attacks are from supernatural beings that have established uninvited emotional entanglements. I am also a target for supernatural beings that have the urge to play god because they have been compromised or tripping as a consequence of being affected by the wrong interpretation of the Christian teachings, a type of poison designed to make the supernatural constitution self-destruct. It is difficult for a supernatural being with a god complex that sees the civil noble lord as someone to be god to, to then adjust to the realization that the civil noble lord is god and not the supernatural constitution according to the correct interpretation of the Christian teachings. These references to my experiences reemphasize the seriousness of the civil right to privacy for the civil noble constitution.

The civil right to self-determination is a sacred right that confirms the civil noble constitution as ruler, a right that forbids supernatural beings from oppressing or dominating the civil noble constitution. This right confirms the civil noble constitution as commissioner of police. Article 3 of the universal declaration of human rights, everyone has the right to life, liberty and security of person. This right authorizes the civil noble lord to create a peace keeping force, a police service, to regulate the behaviour of supernatural beings. This right is not for supernatural beings, it is an expressed right for the civil noble lord, a legal constitution of a person recognized by law.

Article 1 of the international convention on civil and political rights states that all peoples have the right of self-determination. By virtue of that right they freely determine their political status and freely pursue their economic, social and cultural development. This civil right protects the legal person and the legal constitution of the legal person from alteration or compromise by supernatural beings to fit into their unlawful political agenda.

The result of the civil noble constitution exercising the sacred legal right to create a properly constituted police service is that any other police service operating illegally, not properly constituted, promoting and maintaining lawless activities, organized crimes, will be regarded as criminals, they will be disbanded arrested and severely punished. Supernatural crimes are crimes against the state, the civil noble constitution.

If I believe that supernatural beings are engaging in uncivilized activities that might lead to future behavioural problems given the nature of the supernatural constitution in the interest of international peace and security it is my right as a law lord to stop it.

It is unfortunate that because of the wicked nature of the supernatural constitution and as a consequence the organized crimes in the world today that are passed off as governments, to assert my legal rights including the right to life will necessitate a formal declaration of war on all organized crimes in the world today and all types of supernatural political governments.

The nature of the supernatural constitution and the concept of life as a consequence suggests insanity, this makes the defence of life appear to be insane but the effectiveness of good policing is to put aside your personal feelings and to understand that life with all its faults only works with the legal and not the political, how it originally was and not how we might want it to be. There is a thin line between sanity and insanity, love and hate, life and death, war and peace; the only way to avoid the bad is to embrace the legal and not the political, even more so for the political supernatural constitution. The serious mistakes of the susceptible to embrace the political and become insane which appears to be irreversible or unavoidable for everyone create the determination to carry on with the political regardless. This only confirms that the police service must be strong; strength is not political but legal.

The point of policing or the police service is to protect the sacred civil rights of the civil noble constitution, the law, from the insanity of supernatural beings that have adopted self-harm as a lifestyle. This process also establishes peaceful living conditions for supernatural beings that are strong enough to refuse the uncivilized or barbaric urge to self-destruct.

The legitimacy of policing or the police service is the defensive or protective component, the defence or protection of the civil noble constitution, the law, this defensive or protective function can only be achieved with the official identification of the civil noble constitution as the commissioner or the reason, or the purpose. The legitimacy is the civil noble constitution, the law. To avoid supernatural manipulations of this sacred requirement to create a police service for political purposes, there are sacred conditions that must be satisfied, the official identification of the civil noble constitution as commissioner, the reason, with the salary, uniform, and the rights and privileges meant for the civil noble constitution.

I studied in the former Soviet Union for a year, it was demonstrated that the state can provide all necessary services and products like cars for its citizens. These services included restaurants, supermarkets, public transportation, nightclubs, entertainment (television and radio, films and music) etcetera. Effective policing requires the state to provide goods and services for its citizens; it is a fair distribution of the world's resources and eliminates lawlessness. Unfortunately the market economy discriminates, it is political, supernatural, and it favours some to live in luxury while others live in poverty. It is based on a lie and creates the conspiracy to sabotage state services and products. It is a type of conflict or war, survival of the fittest. Some look on seeing others live the billionaire's lifestyle, yachts, and jets expensive cars. It is a thrill for them when people see them with expensive things they cannot afford. They like to be seen with women or men that are out of reached because of how much money they have and they like to be envied.

How do you achieve these objectives with the no working culture that paradise represents? Technological advancements?

Money was a scientific or technological advancement to meet the needs of the world at the world's level of civilization. Money was and still is a very successful scientific invention. Money was an invention to cater to the needs of man, the civil noble constitution, a legal person recognized by law. Money has since its invention been misused or misapplied by supernatural beings that naturally cannot comprehend its usefulness in a civilization and think it is a game to play. The usefulness of money in the world's level of development to the civil noble constitution makes it mandatory that the civil noble constitution must have enough of it to comply with article 3 of the universal declaration of human rights, the right to life.

For purposes of security, policing, supernatural beings must get or acquire things like houses etcetera civilly or orderly through the state, the civil noble constitution, rather than unlawfully supernaturally. It is in everyone's best interest, the civil and supernatural constitutions that the state operates efficiently, effectively.

4. Author's notes

My book racism identifies what real racism is from confusing supernatural simulations. Racism is lawlessness and lawlessness is insanity. Racism is the misuse of supernatural powers and senses to harm the civil noble constitution mentally or physically or to be disruptive or destructive in a real civilized society. It is the direct or indirect persecution of the civil noble constitution, the law, by supernatural beings. This book also identifies the United Nations as an unconstitutional police service, not constituted, incomplete to suit the lawless practices of supernatural beings at the expense of the wellbeing of the vulnerable. The current political purpose of the United Nations violates my legal right under article 3 of the universal declaration of human rights and other legal rights.

It was established from the circumstances that led to the creation of the United Nations during and after the Second World War that you can be of the same skin colour and still be a racist, the Jews and the Nazis, white on white, black on black etcetera. This is a predetermination made regarding real racism the differences between the civil and supernatural constitutions even though of the same skin colour. This confirms that real racism is the unlawful persecution of the civil noble constitution by supernatural beings regardless of skin colour. This also confirms that the civil noble constitution has been identified as a distinct race from the supernatural constitution.

The delicate nature of the civil noble constitution and the hostile nature of the supernatural constitution make the creation of a properly constituted police service an extremely serious matter.

The supernatural constitution is naturally racist because of its hostile nature and the civil noble constitution is not naturally racist because of its civil nature. Policing is about the total elimination of real racism. So is it the civil noble constitution or the supernatural constitution that accomplish this sacred objective?

The United Nations claim to want the interest of all races and cultures in the world represented in the United Nations by representatives of these races and cultures; except the most recognizable, the most important culture and race, the civil noble constitution, the law. This is because of the implications for the current political racist status of the United Nations and lawlessness in the world.

5. Author's biography

My name is Lord Loveday Ememe. I was born in the United Kingdom. I am a graduate of an Anglican seminary school. I graduated from the University of East London with an honours degree in law. I am of a civil noble constitution.

6. Bibliography

The Bible

www.ingramcontent.com/pod-product-compliance
Lightning Source LLC
Chambersburg PA
CBHW072300170526
45158CB00003BA/1124